address book

_____
_____
_____

paperstyle

Copyright © Ryland Peters & Small 2012

Images taken from *Homespun Style* by Selina Lake

Photography by Debi Treloar

copyright © Ryland Peters & Small 2012

Tab divider 'S': frydogdesign.blogspot.com

Published by Paperstyle

20–21 Jockey's Fields, London WC1R 4BW

519 Broadway, 5th Floor, New York NY 10012

www.rylandpeters.com

Printed in China

a

b

👤 .... ☎ ....
....

✉ ....
....
....

@ ....

👤 .... ☎ ....
✉ ....
....
....
....

@ ....

👤 .... ☎ ....
✉ ....
....
....
....

@ ....

👤 .... ☎ ....
✉ ....
....
....
....

@ ....

d

e

f

g

h

ij

k1

m

n

👤 _____   ☎ _____
                                 _____
✉ _____
  _____
  _____
  _____
@ _____

👤 _____   ☎ _____
                                 _____
✉ _____
  _____
  _____
  _____
@ _____

👤 _____   ☎ _____
                                 _____
✉ _____
  _____
  _____
  _____
@ _____

👤 _____   ☎ _____
                                 _____
✉ _____
  _____
  _____
  _____
@ _____

👤 _____   ☎ _____
✉ _____
   _____
   _____
@ _____

👤 _____   ☎ _____
✉ _____
   _____
   _____
@ _____

👤 _____   ☎ _____
✉ _____
   _____
   _____
@ _____

👤 _____   ☎ _____
✉ _____
   _____
   _____
@ _____

pq

S

u v

Wx

♟ _____   ☎ _____
                            _____
✉ _____
  _____
  _____
  _____
@ _____

♟ _____   ☎ _____
                            _____
✉ _____
  _____
  _____
  _____
@ _____

♟ _____   ☎ _____
                            _____
✉ _____
  _____
  _____
  _____
@ _____

♟ _____   ☎ _____
                            _____
✉ _____
  _____
  _____
  _____
@ _____

yz